Original title:
Winter Moon

Copyright © 2024 Swan Charm
All rights reserved.

Author: Daisy Dewi
ISBN HARDBACK: 978-9916-79-996-3
ISBN PAPERBACK: 978-9916-79-997-0
ISBN EBOOK: 978-9916-79-998-7

Hibernation's Muse of Light

In the stillness of the night,
Soft whispers fill the air,
Dreams wrapped in silver light,
Secrets hiding everywhere.

Winter's breath begins to slow,
Blankets woven, deep and warm,
Underneath the falling snow,
Nature's hush, a perfect charm.

Stars gather in the sky,
Like lanterns held with care,
Guiding wanderers nearby,
Through the silence, pure and rare.

Gentle shadows softly creep,
Where the echoes softly play,
In this vast and tranquil sweep,
Night turns slowly into day.

Awake the warmth of dreams unfurled,
Let the heart find peaceful sight,
In the cradle of this world,
Hibernation's muse of light.

Quicksilver in the Underbrush

In shadows deep, where whispers play,
The silver slips, it darts away.
Beneath the leaves, the secrets hide,
A fleeting dance, where dreams collide.

Each rustle speaks of tales untold,
Of fleeting forms, so bright, yet cold.
Like shadows cast by the fading light,
They shimmer brief, then take to flight.

Nature's brush, with strokes of chance,
We watch in awe, a silent trance.
The quicksilver glints with every hue,
In the underbrush, alive, anew.

A Ballet of Light and Shiver

In twilight's grip, the candles sway,
A ballet soft, at close of day.
Each flicker dances, shadows blend,
In every spark, a dream to send.

Through frosted pane, the moonlight streams,
A silver touch on whispered themes.
The air is thick with soft embrace,
Where light and shiver find their place.

A waltz of stars, with whispers sweet,
In silent rhythm, they softly meet.
The heartbeats drum, in sync, alive,
In the dance of night, we thrive.

Ghostly Glimpses of Dim Light

In the stillness, shadows creep,
Ghostly glimpses, secrets keep.
Faintest flickers break the night,
A shimmer lost, beyond our sight.

Specters wander, lost, forlorn,
In dim-lit corners, dreams are born.
They whisper soft, with love's intent,
A haunting song, a life well-spent.

With every pulse, the darkness sighs,
Echoes of life through memories rise.
A tender touch, from realms unseen,
In ghostly light, we drift between.

Radiance in the Icy Embrace

In winter's hold, the world is still,
A radiance glows on the hill.
Crystal shimmers on branches bare,
In icy arms, a beauty rare.

The frosty breath, so crisp and clear,
Whispers tales for all to hear.
Each flake that falls, a diamond bright,
In nature's grasp, purest delight.

A silent gaze, as stars appear,
In the icy night, we draw near.
With every chill, a warmth we find,
In the embrace of winter's kind.

Nightfall's Crystal Crown

The stars ignite the velvet night,
Each shimmer holds a tale so bright.
Whispers of dreams in the cool breeze,
A world awash in silver seas.

Moonlit paths softly unwind,
Guiding hearts that seek and find.
With every step, the shadows play,
As night conquers the fading day.

In the stillness, secrets bloom,
Casting away the day's old gloom.
A crown of crystals, pure delight,
Adorns the earth in gentle light.

Through the quiet, time stands still,
As stars lace dreams with winter chill.
In this realm of wonder, free,
Nightfall sings sweet harmony.

Soft Grasp of the Frosted Ether

In the cradle of frost laid bare,
Nature breathes a tender care.
Each flake a whisper, gentle flight,
Dancing in the soft, pale light.

Veils of mist, like secrets spun,
Wrap the world till day is done.
Hushed are cries, as twilight calls,
In the ether, magic falls.

Stars emerge in frozen air,
Glistening gems beyond compare.
Softly, softly, the silence flows,
In the stillness, beauty grows.

Trees wear coats of frosty lace,
Embracing winter's cold embrace.
In this realm, lost in the night,
Lies a tender, quiet light.

Tranquil Beams on Frozen Earth

Beneath the surface, stillness reigns,
In frozen fields where silence remains.
Sunlight dances, soft and shy,
Kissing the ground, a gentle sigh.

Tranquil beams weave through the frost,
Whispers of warmth in chill embossed.
Nature holds its breath so tight,
In the embrace of soft twilight.

Each shadow long and fleeting bends,
Where day and night do softly blend.
Life sleeps beneath the icy crust,
In time's tender, patient trust.

Hope glimmers, faint but clear,
In the heart, the warmth draws near.
Frozen landscapes, bright as day,
Reveal the dreams that softly lay.

Elysium under Hushed Skies

In Elysium, the quiet sings,
Under skies where soft light clings.
Whispers of winds weave through trees,
Carrying tales of ancient seas.

Petals fall like fragrant dreams,
Flowing gently in silver streams.
Stars awaken, one by one,
As playful shadows start to run.

Clouds drift lazily, soft and white,
Brushing against the edge of night.
In this haven, souls take flight,
And bask in the glow of fading light.

Boundless joy in tranquil space,
Life flourishes with gentle grace.
In this realm where dreams collapse,
Elysium waits with open laps.

Night's Soft Glare

Under stars, the world stands still,
Gentle breezes give a thrill.
Moonlight dances on the ground,
Whispers of the night abound.

Shadows play on velvet grass,
As time flows, moments pass.
Crickets sing their lullaby,
Night's embrace, a sweet sigh.

Clouds drift softly, silver bright,
Hiding secrets out of sight.
Each twinkle tells a story old,
In this warmth, the night unfolds.

Close your eyes, let dreams take flight,
In this realm, all feels right.
Heartbeats match the evening's song,
In the stillness, we belong.

With every breath, the night renews,
Painting skies in deeper blues.
In night's soft glare, we find our peace,
A quiet joy that will not cease.

Crystal Reflections in the Dark

In the stillness, silence speaks,
Crystal visions, beauty peaks.
Moonlit pools like mirrors gleam,
Echoes weave a fragile dream.

Every ripple tells a tale,
Of whispered winds and softest wail.
Stars dip low in water's gaze,
Life refracts in shimmering ways.

In the depths, the secrets hide,
With each breath, the shadows bide.
Crystal prisms catch the light,
As the dark surrenders night.

Hold your thoughts, let silence flow,
In the dark, we learn to grow.
Reflections whisper, calm and clear,
Echoes of the heart we hear.

So linger long by waters deep,
In these crystals, secrets keep.
What was lost may yet return,
In their shimmer, fire will burn.

Lanterns of a Chill Night

Lanterns flicker, warm and bright,
Guiding hearts through chilly night.
Softly glowing, shadows weave,
In their light, we dare believe.

Each lantern tells a story told,
Of dreams pursued and hopes bold.
Huddled close, with friends we share,
In the glow, we shed our care.

Fragrant breezes swirl around,
Nature's breath, a tender sound.
As laughter dances in the air,
With every flicker, love's laid bare.

Beneath the dome of starlit sky,
With glowing lanterns, spirits fly.
Embers warm, our hearts ignite,
In the silence, all feels right.

So we wander through the night,
Lanterns glowing, hearts in flight.
Every step, a rhythm found,
In the chill, our souls unbound.

Mirror of the Frozen Heart

In the stillness, ice forms clear,
A mirror shows what we hold dear.
Frozen whispers, secrets kept,
In this chill, our truths are swept.

Each shard a story, jagged, bright,
Reflecting shadows of the night.
In this crystal, we see inside,
Where warmth and silence often bide.

Beneath the frost, a fire burns,
Yearning speaks, our spirit yearns.
A frozen heart, yet full of dreams,
Glowing softly, hope still beams.

Hold this mirror close and tight,
See the darkness, feel the light.
In its depths, find who you are,
A glimmered soul, a shining star.

So as winter wraps its cloak,
Let this mirror shift and stoke.
For in the cold, the heart will find,
A warmth that speaks to every mind.

Frost-kissed Dreams Unraveled

In the stillness of the morn,
Dreams like whispers gently born,
Frost unfolds on every leaf,
A shimmering, icy brief.

Voices call from far away,
Echoes of a brighter day,
Hope dances in the glinting light,
Chasing shadows of the night.

Beneath the sky's soft, silver hue,
Wonders wrapped in shades of blue,
Every breath a crystal sigh,
As winter's magic passes by.

Each step taken on this ground,
Crackling sounds, a soothing sound,
Threads of ice weave through the air,
Wrap my heart like tender care.

Yet in this chill, warmth still gleams,
Frost-kissed dreams, like gentle streams,
Flow through moments, crystal clear,
Whispering that spring is near.

Glimmering Frost on Sleek Boughs

Dewdrops cling to boughs so sleek,
Glimmering like treasures unique,
Winter's breath in sparkles gleams,
    Nature's art in icy themes.

Silence reigns, the world holds breath,
    In this hush, a dance with death,
Each branch dressed in crystal lace,
A fleeting glimpse of time and space.

    Underneath the moon's embrace,
      Frosty patterns interlace,
    Delicate, the night unfolds,
Secrets wrapped in silver folds.

Stars above like diamonds shine,
    Illuminating shadows fine,
    In this night, a tale is spun,
Of frost and dreams, two intertwined.

Beneath the weight of winter's crown,
The glimmering frost won't back down,
    Beauty found in cold repose,
Where even silence softly glows.

Nymphs in the Frigid Gleam

In the glimmer of the frost,
Nymphs dance where the warmth was lost,
Whispers float on icy air,
Children of the winter's care.

Through the branches, laughter twirls,
As the snow gently unfurls,
Their soft steps, a ghostly trace,
Woven in a fragile grace.

Glistening in soft moonlight,
Nymphs weave dreams in silver night,
With each flicker, stories flow,
Of magic born in winter's glow.

In the hush of midnight's haze,
They sing songs of frozen days,
Their allure, a fleeting spark,
Guiding hearts through winters dark.

Yet time shifts, as seasons change,
Nymphs will fade, the world rearrange,
But their essence lingers still,
In every echo, every chill.

Celestial Glow Through Branches Bare

Amidst the branches, stark and bare,
A glow descends, a light so rare,
Celestial whispers in the night,
Paint the world in purest white.

Stars align in perfect gleam,
Frigid skies that spark and dream,
Through the wood, a gentle sigh,
As night unveils the winter sky.

Echoes of a soft refrain,
Crafted in the winter's vein,
Dancing lights with passion flare,
Spellbound hearts caught unaware.

Underneath the heavens vast,
Moments fleeting, shadows cast,
In this dream of frost and night,
Life's entwined in pure delight.

Celestial glow, like silver threads,
Weaving tales, where love yet spreads,
Through branches bare, a promise made,
In winter's heart, bright dreams won't fade.

The Chill of Forgotten Tales

In the shadows of the night,
Whispers drift, a ghostly flight.
Stories buried, lost in time,
Echo softly, rhyme by rhyme.

Beneath the frost of ancient trees,
Secrets carried by the breeze.
Frozen moments, tales untold,
In the silence, they unfold.

Brittle pages, worn and thin,
Memories linger, deep within.
Chill of echoes grips the air,
Fables linger everywhere.

Through the mist, the figures roam,
Searching still for words of home.
Time stands still, it holds its breath,
In the grip of quiet death.

Winter's hush, a sacred space,
In the chill, a soft embrace.
Forgotten tales, both dark and bright,
Savoring the taste of night.

Celestial Frost in Motion

Stars awake in velvet skies,
Whispers of the night arise.
Silver trails of cosmic dust,
In the chill, the dreams are thrust.

Moonlight dances on the lake,
Waves of frost that gently break.
Celestial bodies intertwine,
In their glow, the shadows shine.

Snowflakes twirl in wild delight,
Carried on the breath of night.
Each one tells a story new,
In the stillness, magic's view.

Galaxies in silent grace,
Traveling through the endless space.
Frosted air, a breath of peace,
In the freeze, our worries cease.

As the dawn begins to rise,
Crisp and clear, revealing ties.
Motion in a world reborn,
Celestial frost, a new dawn's morn.

Illuminated by the Crisp Dawn

Morning breaks with gentle hues,
Light spills forth with morning's news.
Frosty air, so fresh and bright,
Wrapped in warmth, the world ignites.

Horizon kissed by sun's first rays,
Softly lighting winter's ways.
Each blade glistens, diamonds pure,
A tranquil moment, wild and sure.

Birds awaken, song in flight,
Echoing the pure delight.
Embers of a night-long dream,
Born anew in sunlight's gleam.

In the chill, a warmth ignites,
Glowing hopes of future sights.
Crisp and clear, the day unfolds,
In its hands, a tale it molds.

Illuminated hearts will soar,
Chasing dreams forevermore.
In the dawn, our spirits rise,
Painting joy across the skies.

Serenity Wrapped in Silver Light

Night enveloped in silver dew,
Calmness drapes the earth anew.
Gentle whispers soothe the trees,
Wrapped in peace, a fragile breeze.

Stars like lanterns in the dark,
Guiding us with every spark.
Nature holds her breath in grace,
In this stillness, we embrace.

Moonbeams play upon the ground,
In this magic, silence found.
Softly, quietly, hearts will mend,
In the light, our souls descend.

Wrapped in layers of the night,
Dreams will linger, pure and bright.
Serenity within our reach,
In silver light, the world will teach.

As the night gives way to dawn,
Echoes of the day are drawn.
In each moment, hearts unite,
Serenity wrapped in silver light.

Ghostly Mirage of Light

Whispers of shadows float in the night,
Dancing reflections in flickering light.
Echoes of dreams in a shimmering haze,
Lost in the moment, a spectral phase.

Through silvered mists where the moon does gleam,
Reality wavers, a silken dream.
Footsteps of phantoms in twilight's embrace,
Weaving their tales through an endless space.

Fragments of time held in fleeting sight,
Glimmers of hope shining ever so bright.
Chasing the echoes, we wander astray,
Drawn to the mysteries that call us to play.

Silent the forest, beneath starlit skies,
Fleeting connections, where heartache lies.
Guided by visions that pulse in the dark,
We seek that moment, that flickering spark.

In ghostly mirages, our spirits take flight,
Bound to the beauty that glimmers in night.
Lost in the charm of this luminous sight,
Forever entranced by the ghostly light.

Shrouded in Frosted Euphoria

Awake in a world draped in crystalline gleam,
Each breath a whisper, each moment a dream.
Frosted enchantments weave tales in the air,
Shrouded in euphoria, everywhere.

Silvery branches, a laughter of ice,
Sparkling diamonds in nature's precise.
Shadows and mysteries meld into glow,
Carving a pathway where few dare to go.

Chasing the echoes, embracing the chill,
Hearts intertwining as time stands still.
Capturing whispers of joy on the breeze,
Wrapped in the warmth that visions appease.

Glinting reflections in delicate grace,
Moments of magic that softly embrace.
Shrouded in wonder, we twirl and we play,
Lost in the beauty of frost-kissed ballet.

As sunlight fades, and night draws near,
Frosted euphoria, a vision so clear.
In silence we linger, in harmony sway,
Shrouded forever in winter's ballet.

Light's Lull in Dusk's Embrace

Dimmed by the twilight, the day finds its rest,
Colors entwining, as if they were blessed.
Fading to whispers, the light starts to hum,
Wrapped in the stillness, the night's gentle drum.

Golden horizons dissolve into blue,
Painting the heavens with delicate hue.
Stars hold their breath in the velvet of night,
Cradling secrets, hidden from sight.

Cool breezes whisper, and time seems to pause,
Embracing the magic, the world's gentle cause.
Moments of clarity linger and then,
Drifting like clouds, they return once again.

In this sweet lull, where dreams intertwine,
Softly we wander, through shadows divine.
Cascading whispers, the dusk calls our name,
Echoes of stories, forever the same.

Light's lull in dusk, a tender caress,
Capturing hearts in a soft, warm embrace.
Here in this magic, we breathe and we sigh,
Wrapped in the wonder beneath the night sky.

A Dance of the Frosted Spheres

Twilight descends with a silvery glow,
Frosted spheres dancing, as if with a flow.
Glittering crystals in rhythm align,
Nature's sweet symphony, so pure and divine.

Swirling in circles, the whispers of fate,
Bound by the moment, we glide and await.
Steps interwoven in breezes so light,
Carried by echoes of day turning night.

In the soft glow, we twirl and we spin,
Lost in the laughter, the warmth from within.
Frigid caresses, the moon's tender kiss,
Euphoria's promise in this frozen bliss.

As shadows lengthen and soft shadows play,
Time melts away in this magical ballet.
Frosted orbs twinkle, as stars start to gleam,
Carried in laughter, we lose track of dreams.

A dance of the spheres, in delicate flight,
Lifting our spirits, igniting the night.
Held in the moment, we cherish the view,
As frosted spheres shimmer, forever anew.

Frosty Silver Glow

Moonlit whispers touch the ground,
A silver glow, serene and round.
Chill of night wraps dreams in lace,
Nature sleeps with gentle grace.

Softly sighs the crystal air,
Snowflakes dance without a care.
Each glimmer sparkles, pure delight,
In this calm and frosty night.

Trees adorned in icy gleam,
Frozen branches softly dream.
In the silence, hearts will know,
Peaceful thoughts in silver glow.

Stars above begin to fade,
While the moon's bright path is laid.
Winter's hush, a sacred rite,
Cradles all in sweet twilight.

Time stands still in this embrace,
Frosty whispers set the pace.
Underneath the starry show,
Life flows gently, soft and slow.

The Pale Embrace of Night

Shadows stretch beneath the trees,
Carried by a whispering breeze.
With a touch of starlit grace,
Night enfolds us, soft embrace.

Silvery mists, they softly creep,
Cradling dreams while we still sleep.
In the dark, each thought takes flight,
Guided by the pale moonlight.

Time drifts gently, calm and slow,
In the arms of night's soft glow.
Silence weaves a tender thread,
Binding hearts where hopes are bred.

Echoes of the day now fade,
In this quiet serenade.
Wrapped in night's familiar shroud,
We find solace, lost yet proud.

Here we breathe the silent air,
Moments linger, pure and rare.
In the pale embrace of night,
All our worries take their flight.

Ethereal Winter's Lullaby

Snowflakes fall like whispered dreams,
Waltzing softly, bright moonbeams.
In the hush of winter's night,
Nature hums a tune of light.

Branches sway in frozen grace,
While the stars keep watchful pace.
Crystals twinkle, pure and bright,
Ethereal in the still of night.

Blankets woven, white and deep,
Cradling earth in gentle sleep.
Here the world finds rest, so slow,
To the song of winter's flow.

Voices of the night arise,
Carried softly through the skies.
Melodies of peace and cheer,
Filling hearts, drawing them near.

In this place, time stands anew,
Each moment draped in silver hue.
Ethereal whispers softly sigh,
Winter's gentle lullaby.

Celestial Chill

Stars above, a million eyes,
Watching over as night flies.
In the dark, a chill so sweet,
Dancing lightly on our feet.

Frosty breath of cosmic light,
Cradles dreams throughout the night.
Winds weave songs of ancient lore,
Calling us to seek and explore.

Every flake, a tale untold,
Shimmering in the night so bold.
In this vast celestial sea,
We find wonder, wild and free.

Night unfolds with tender grace,
As the stars begin to trace.
Celestial chill wraps us tight,
Guiding souls through the starlight.

Resting hearts in tranquil space,
Feel the universe's embrace.
In the silence, dreams fulfill,
Lost in wonder, celestial chill.

Nocturnal Reverie in Cold Embrace

In the stillness of the night,
Whispers dance in pale moonlight.
Dreams take flight, shadows sway,
Wrapped in frost, where silence lay.

Stars like diamonds, twinkle bright,
Casting echoes, soft and slight.
Thoughts unravel, gently weave,
Lost in dreams, we dare believe.

In the chill, our spirits roam,
Through the darkness, we find home.
Embraced by night's tender hand,
Together in this mystic land.

Cold winds sing a haunting tune,
Beneath the glow of silver moon.
In the dreams we find our grace,
Nocturnal echoes, cold embrace.

Let the night forever stay,
Guiding us till break of day.
In this realm where dreams are spun,
We are many, yet we're one.

Éclat in a Burden of Snow

Falling softly, white and pure,
Snowflakes whisper, thoughts obscure.
Blankets thick upon the ground,
Winter's hush, a world unbound.

Glistening paths where shadows play,
Footsteps fade, then slip away.
Underneath the frosty veil,
Silent tales in shadows sail.

Éclat gleams in winter's light,
Dreams aglow, hearts take flight.
Each flake serves a tale anew,
In the hush, we find our view.

Burdened trees in silver crowned,
Nature's breath, a sacred sound.
In the quiet, solace found,
Whispers echo all around.

Breathe in deep, let worries freeze,
In this moment, find your ease.
Together in the snow we stroll,
Finding warmth in winter's soul.

Embrace of the Celestial Chill

Upon the night, a blanket laid,
Stars emerge, the darkness played.
Celestial beams in quiet grace,
Whisper secrets, time and space.

Moonlight bathes the world in glow,
Caressing softly, cool and slow.
Hearts entwined in cosmic trance,
Underneath the night's romance.

Chill of air, a breath so sweet,
Nature's song, a rhythmic beat.
In the vast, we find our place,
Embrace the night, the void we chase.

Frozen stillness all around,
Magic in the hush profound.
In the chill, our spirits soar,
Bound to stars, forevermore.

Here we stand, two souls aligned,
Lost in time, the world confined.
In this embrace of endless night,
We are one, a cosmic light.

Silent Silver Glow

Morning breaks with muted grace,
Silver dreams in soft embrace.
Gentle whispers, shadows fade,
In the light, new paths are laid.

Clouds drift softly, skies aglow,
A world reborn in silent flow.
Magic lingers in the air,
Quiet moments filled with care.

Nature still, in peace we find,
Harmony that ties the mind.
Each soft hue, a brush of calm,
In this stillness, like a balm.

Silent glances, hearts unite,
Underneath the pale twilight.
Together we walk this road,
Where the silver sun bestowed.

In this space, let dreams revive,
With the morning, we arrive.
In the glow, we find our way,
Silent silver guides the day.

A Silvery Veil Overhead

A silvery veil overhead, so bright,
Whispers of dreams take silent flight.
Stars twinkle softly, a waltz in the night,
Under the moon's kiss, a tranquil light.

Echoes of laughter drift through the air,
Memories linger, they float everywhere.
The world is aglow, a magical sight,
A canvas of wonders, wrapped up tight.

Snowflakes descend like delicate lace,
Covering earth in a soft embrace.
Nature's embrace, serene and pure,
In this moment, I feel so sure.

Glimmers of joy in each gentle flake,
Carving our path, frozen lakes awake.
A symphony plays on this winter's stage,
Life in its stillness, a heart's warm page.

As night dances on with graceful ease,
Under the stars, my spirit finds peace.
A silvery veil, a comforting shroud,
In the arms of the night, I stand proud.

Gleaming Under the Cold Ink

Under cold ink, the night starts to gleam,
Stars scatter like whispers, a lucid dream.
Shadows dance lightly, a quiet ballet,
In the hush of the eve, we drift and sway.

Each breath feels crisp, each moment is still,
Silence embraces, a soft, tender thrill.
Frost on the ground, a delicate trace,
Marking the journey, time's gentle grace.

The world catches shimmer, reflections ignite,
Glistening softly in the pale moonlight.
A world painted white, serene and divine,
In this fleeting moment, forever is mine.

Whispers of breezes weave through the night,
Caressing each heart, making spirits bright.
Cocooned in the stillness, I find my place,
Gleaming under the cold, a warm embrace.

Dancing like stardust, dreams intermingle,
In the quiet of night, my thoughts softly tingle.
The ink of the sky, vast and profound,
Gleams evermore in this silence unbound.

The Frozen Tapestry of Night

A frozen tapestry unfolds with grace,
Stars scatter like jewels in endless space.
The sky wears a cloak of midnight dreams,
Where whispers of magic dance and gleam.

Cradled in shadows, secrets reside,
The hush of the night, a faith confide.
Snowflakes weave stories, old and new,
In the winter's embrace, we start anew.

The air carries notes of sweet, silken chill,
As whispers of winter, the heart they fill.
Each moment unfurls like a silken thread,
Draped over time, where all fears are shed.

Candles are flickering, warmth in the dark,
Illuminating dreams that flame with a spark.
In this frozen realm, we're wrapped in light,
Breath of serenity tames the long night.

Eclipsed by the beauty that nature deploys,
The tapestry shimmers, erasing all noise.
Bonfires of wonder burn brightly and bright,
In the still of the dark, we take flight.

Halo of Winter's Breathe

In the stillness, a halo begins to glow,
Winter's breath whispers beneath the snow.
Crisp air carries tales from yesteryears,
Echoing softly, it calms all fears.

Beneath the white canvas, dreams gently weave,
In the heart of the night, we learn to believe.
Stars hang like lanterns, illuminating the dark,
Guiding the wanderer's silent heart's spark.

Branches are laden with crystalline lace,
Embracing the beauty of nature's embrace.
Each flake a wish, tenderly spun,
Kissing the earth, as two hearts become one.

Light dances on edges, the moon finds her throne,
Yes, under this halo, we're never alone.
Breath visible, lingering in the cold,
Winter's sweet story continues to unfold.

As twilight whispers the promise of dawn,
In this serene moment, our worries are gone.
Wrapped in a halo of winter's pure grace,
Together, forever, we find our place.

Radiance in the Frozen Sky

Beneath the shimmering veil of night,
Stars whisper secrets in silver light.
The frost on branches, a crystal dream,
Dances gently, a winter's gleam.

The moon hangs low, a guardian bright,
Casting shadows that surge and fight.
Whispers of wind through the silent trees,
A symphony played with chilling ease.

Auroras swirl, a heavenly show,
In icy realms where cold winds blow.
Nature's canvas, a vibrant sight,
Radiance dances in the frozen night.

Softly it glows, the snowflakes fall,
Each one reflecting the night's call.
A tapestry woven with threads of light,
Emboldened spirits take joyful flight.

In this embrace, all worries freeze,
Finding solace in chilly breeze.
The beauty lingers, forever nigh,
Radiance glows in the frozen sky.

Night's Icy Lantern

A lantern flickers in the midnight air,
Casting shadows, a mystical flare.
The chill of dusk wraps all around,
While whispers in silence seem to abound.

Footprints crunch on the powdery floor,
Guided by light, we seek for more.
Each step etched in a frosty blend,
Where time stands still, no start or end.

The stars above twinkle with might,
A celestial map in the velvet night.
Night's icy lantern, a beacon bold,
Illuminates tales yet to be told.

Beneath the glow of this crystal sphere,
We find a warmth that draws us near.
In the vast expanse, our hearts ignite,
Lost in the wonder of the night.

With every breath, the chill revives,
As we wander through the frozen lives.
Night's icy lantern, forever shine,
Guiding our souls through realms divine.

A Glimmer upon the Snow

A whispering breeze on a quiet eve,
Holds secrets in snowflakes, hard to believe.
Each glimmer dances, a fleeting guest,
A tale of wonder in winter's nest.

Crystalline jewels upon the ground,
Sparkle and shine where quiet is found.
Soft footprints weave through moonlit rows,
A path of dreams where magic flows.

The stillness sings in the frost-kissed air,
While shadows linger in a moonlit lair.
A glimmer resides in the depths of night,
A promise held in the heart's soft light.

Glistening chills wrap around the trees,
As magic lingers on the winter's breeze.
In every sparkle, a story is spun,
Of hopes awakened, of dreams begun.

With every breath, the season awakes,
Through shimmering veils, the stillness shakes.
A glimmer remains, pure and bright,
In the quiet embrace of the snowy night.

Ghostly Gleam

In the hush of twilight, shadows blend,
A ghostly gleam that whispers and bends.
Through the barren branches, stories flow,
Of memories captured in moonlit glow.

The air turns cold as echoes reign,
In the haunted dance of joy and pain.
Figures of old, in silken white,
Drift through the silence of the starry night.

Frosted breath hangs, crisp and clear,
As specters drift near, ever so dear.
A tale unfolds in the frosty gleam,
Awakening dreams from a starlit dream.

With each step taken on winter's breath,
We follow the spirits that whisper of death.
Yet joy lingers in shadows of past,
In ghostly gleams that eternally last.

The night wraps tight in a tranquil embrace,
As ghostly forms weave in an ethereal lace.
In the quiet, we find truth reside,
In the ghostly gleam, life's tender guide.

The Chill That Sings

Whispers in the frosty air,
Cool winds weave a gentle snare.
Melodies of winter's breath,
Haunting notes of quiet death.

Snowflakes dance like fleeting dreams,
Lurking shadows stir the streams.
In the night, the world holds still,
Nature's songs, a solemn thrill.

Branches crack with every sigh,
Underneath a ghostly sky.
Crisp and clear the echoes flow,
In the chill, our hearts will glow.

Listen to the silence call,
Each sharp note a fleeting fall.
Memories of summer past,
In the cold, too sweet to last.

Yet in stillness, warmth may grow,
In the heart, a gentle glow.
Through the chill, we will take wing,
For in winter's chill, we sing.

Glistening Secrets of the Night

Moonbeams shimmer on the lake,
Mirrors of the stars they make.
Secrets whispered in the trees,
Floating softly on the breeze.

Glistening shadows softly creep,
While the world is fast asleep.
Dreams are woven, dusk to dawn,
As night unveils its velvet fawn.

Crickets chirp their evening tune,
Beneath the watchful, silver moon.
Each sound a story to be told,
In the night, their charms unfold.

Fireflies twinkle like lost souls,
Guiding wanderers with their goals.
Magic lingers in the dark,
A whispered promise leaves its mark.

Awake, the world holds breath and waits,
For dawn to clear the night's debates.
In twilight's grip, dreams take flight,
In glistening secrets of the night.

Echoes Beneath the Stars

Starlight spills on tranquil waves,
Echoes of the night, it saves.
Whispers dance on silver tides,
Where mysteries and magic hides.

Galaxies unravel slow,
Painting tales in muted glow.
In the dark, our thoughts collide,
Carried forth on cosmic tide.

Each heartbeat feels like timeless grace,
In the night, we find our place.
Voices lost in endless space,
Drawn together, time's embrace.

Comets streak with fiery trails,
Wishing hopes in silent gales.
Every glance, a promise sworn,
In the dark, new dreams are born.

Boundless realms of endless night,
Guide our hearts to find the light.
Forevermore, we roam with stars,
Echoes beneath, no more bars.

Ethereal Frost on Flickering Flames

In the glow of twilight's ember,
Frosty dreams in silence tremble.
Softly, softly, sparks will rise,
Underneath the twilight skies.

Flames that flicker dance and sway,
Chasing shadows from the day.
Ethereal frost, a purest gleam,
Capturing the heart's deep dream.

Breath of winter, crisp and bright,
Sings a song of starry night.
Each flicker tells a story clear,
Of forgotten hopes, drawing near.

In this warmth, the cold we face,
Meets the gentle, tender grace.
Spirits rise with every breath,
Bound together in this quest.

Together, flames and frost will blend,
A love that time cannot suspend.
In the dance of night and day,
Ethereal frost leads the way.

Moonlit Frost's Teardrop

Under the glimmering night,
Frost drapes the slumbering fields.
A teardrop hangs with grace,
Captured in moon's soft light.

Whispers of winter's breath,
Evoke the quiet calm.
Stars twinkle in bemusement,
As shadows sway in dreams.

Nature holds its secret,
In the chill of ghostly air.
Each sparkle tells a story,
Of moments lost in time.

The world lies hushed and still,
Beneath the silver gaze.
Embrace the fleeting beauty,
Of frost's soft, tender tear.

In the echo of silence,
Magic weaves its art.
A dance of light and shadows,
Filling hearts with wonder.

A Solitary Dance of Light

In the twilight's tender hush,
A single glow takes flight.
It twirls upon the surface,
A solitary dance of light.

Each spark ignites the darkness,
Guiding the lost and meek.
In the labyrinth of shadows,
It whispers without a peak.

A luminous companion,
Through valleys deep and wide.
It beckons to the weary,
With arms open, untied.

Underneath the endless sky,
The stars begin to hum.
Their chorus fills the silence,
A cadence to overcome.

In this shimmering expanse,
Hope flickers like the flame.
A solitary dance for all,
Will never be the same.

Absence and Presence in the Frigid Night

In the cold of moonlit gloom,
Absence lingers like a sigh.
Yet presence hides in shadows,
A warmth that never dies.

The stillness breathes a story,
Of love shaped by the breeze.
Each branch bears silent witness,
To what the heart believes.

Footprints left in soft white snow,
Whisper of those who roam.
Each mark a fleeting memory,
A path that leads us home.

The night holds sacred secrets,
Where echoes softly ring.
A dance of absence present,
In every fluttered wing.

As frost clings to the windows,
Inside, our spirits glow.
In absence and in presence,
Love's fire will always grow.

Dreams Woven in Crystal Threads

In the realm of quiet dreams,
Crystals scatter light unseen.
Each glimmer tells a story,
Of wonders yet to glean.

A tapestry of stardust,
Woven with hope and time.
Each thread a whispered promise,
In the silence, a chime.

Through the night, we wander slow,
Chasing shadows on the ground.
With every step, creation,
In our hearts, is profound.

The frosted air embraces,
Dreams that gently glide.
Invisible connections,
In the stillness, abide.

Awake in soft reflections,
As dawn begins to sing.
By day we spin our stories,
In the light, our hopes take wing.

A Parable of Frosted Nights

In the hush of winter's breath,
Whispers dance on icy ground,
Moonlight spills like molten gold,
Tales of nights where dreams are found.

Each flake tells a tale of time,
Carved in silver, soft and light,
Hidden lore beneath the chill,
A parable of frost and night.

Trees adorned in crystal gowns,
Stand as sentinels so wise,
Guardians of the quiet dreams,
Beneath the vast and twinkling skies.

As shadows drape the sleeping world,
Stars begin their silent flight,
Guiding hearts through coldest dark,
In the warmth of thoughts ignited bright.

When dawn breaks with softest hues,
A canvas brushed with warmth and cheer,
The frost will melt, but tales remain,
In every heart, forever near.

Gentle Crystals in the Gloom

Gentle crystals in the gloom,
Glistening like scattered dreams,
Covering earth in frozen peace,
Crafting worlds of silent themes.

Each morning brings a fresh delight,
Softly kissing the slumbering earth,
Awakening beneath the light,
A symphony of frosty birth.

Whispers travel on winter air,
Carried on a chilly breeze,
Secrets held in fragile hands,
Amongst the swaying frosted trees.

In shadows where the chill resides,
A quiet hope begins to rise,
For even in the coldest nights,
Spring awaits beneath the skies.

So let the crystals weave their spell,
In every corner, every room,
For even in this frosted spell,
A heart can find its way to bloom.

Whispers Beneath the Quiet Stars

Whispers beneath the quiet stars,
Echo softly through the night,
Carried by the whispering winds,
Wrapped in blankets of soft light.

The world is still, yet hearts beat loud,
Underneath the shimmering sky,
Dreams take flight like distant birds,
Rising high, they dare to fly.

Crickets sing their nightly song,
Accompanied by rustling leaves,
In the shadows, secrets dance,
In every sigh, the night believes.

Stars twinkle with ancient tales,
Crafted through the eons long,
Guiding seekers wandering lost,
To find their place where they belong.

As dawn beckons with golden hues,
A gentle promise lingers near,
That even in the darkest times,
New hopes rise, each day sincere.

A Night Frosted and Bright

A night frosted and bright,
Shimmering under the vast expanse,
Where echoes linger in the cold,
Inviting hearts to join the dance.

The silver moon, a watchful eye,
Casts her glow on paths unknown,
While whispers of the frozen breeze,
Carry stories in gentle tone.

Each flake that falls, a unique song,
Painting silence with every breath,
Nature's canvas, pure and strong,
A testament of life and death.

Stars ignite the canvas above,
Guiding dreams on a chilly tide,
While worlds beneath the frost unfold,
In night's embrace, love does abide.

As dawn approaches with gentle grace,
The frost dissolves, yet memories cling,
A night frosted and bright remains,
In heart's delight, forever spring.

An Enigma Wrapped in Frost

In shadows deep, the mystery glows,
Whispers of winter, where nobody goes.
A lace of ice on secrets laid bare,
Veils of frost in the crisp evening air.

Silent paths where the echoes creep,
Nature's riddle, a promise to keep.
Beneath the chill, the warmth hides away,
An enigma lingers at the end of the day.

Crystals gleam under the silver light,
Questions arise in the midst of the night.
Each breath reveals a story untold,
Wrapped in frost, in a silence so bold.

Time dances slow on the frozen stream,
Fragments of reality blend with a dream.
A moment captured, a thought on the breeze,
An enigma that flutters and fades with the freeze.

The Softest Glow of the Cold

The twilight whispers a gentle refrain,
As frost-kissed leaves adorn the terrain.
A soft embrace of the evening's breath,
Where silence blooms in the hush of death.

Stars twinkle shyly in the deepening blue,
Illuminating paths where shadows once grew.
An ethereal glow paints the world white,
In this stillness, the heart takes flight.

Time's drifting hand casts a tender spell,
In the crispness of love that words cannot tell.
The softest glow in the world of the cold,
Whispers of warmth in the stories retold.

Each breath syncs with the night's gentle sigh,
As dreams take root under the vast, starry sky.
A tapestry woven of light and of shade,
Unraveled softly, where memories fade.

Reflections on a Chilled Surface

Glistening mirrors on a frozen pond,
Reflecting moments, a quiet bond.
Each ripple whispers a tale of the past,
Echoes of laughter, fleeting and fast.

In the stillness, the world seems anew,
Beneath the surface, where secrets brew.
Dancing shadows on the icy expanse,
Hold stories of life in a delicate trance.

The chill of the air brings clarity near,
As reflections shimmer, the vision stays clear.
A fleeting glimpse of what once was bright,
Now trapped in the cold, devoid of light.

Frozen in time, the moments remain,
An artwork sculpted by winter's domain.
In the crystal depths, we search for our dreams,
As reflections swirl in the quietest streams.

Harbinger of Frosty Dreams

The dawn breaks softly with a shivering grace,
Heralding dreams in a glistening space.
A chill in the air, like a whispered refrain,
The harbinger comes with an icy champagne.

Each frost-laden branch holds a promise untold,
Of visions that shimmer, of stories of old.
The world awakens with a delicate sigh,
As frosty dreams dance in the pale morning sky.

In this quiet moment, possibilities bloom,
With the light that breaks through the shadows and gloom.

A tapestry woven with frost and with light,
A harbinger calling to take flight tonight.

With every heartbeat, the winter unveils,
A journey unfurling on delicate trails.
Let the frost be our guide, ushering in,
A world full of dreams where the new day begins.

Fractured Light on Icy Grounds

Shards of sun on frozen earth,
Whispers of a fragile birth.
Glistening beneath a pale sky,
Silent dreams as moments fly.

Every crack a story's trace,
In this cold, a warm embrace.
Fragments dance in fleeting hues,
Nature's voice, a muted muse.

Twilight casts a shadow's dare,
Footsteps softened, unaware.
Through the winter's silent veil,
Hopeful hearts begin to sail.

Brittle branches, tales unfold,
In the frost, the brave and bold.
Against the chill, they rise and bend,
In this stillness, spirits mend.

Fractured visions come alive,
In the ice, the echoes thrive.
Glimmers from the depth of night,
Binding shadows with the light.

The Hidden Script of Cold

In the winter's quiet hold,
Lies a tale, a script of cold.
Lines of frost on window panes,
Secrets whispered in the rains.

Beneath the surface, whispers creep,
In the still, where silence sleeps.
Symbols carved by nature's hand,
Understand the frost-kissed land.

Pages turn as breezes sigh,
While the clouds drift softly by.
Reading shadows in the white,
Finding warmth within the night.

Frigid breaths in icy air,
Stories woven, rare and fair.
Every flake holds truth untold,
In the quiet, brave and bold.

Hidden thoughts like snowflakes fall,
Softly resting, heeding all.
In the cold, we find our place,
A connection, a warm embrace.

Hushed Echoes Amongst Barren Trees

In the stillness, whispers glide,
Barren branches, shadows wide.
Hushed echoes in the evening air,
Nature's silence, calm and rare.

Roots entwined in frozen earth,
Holding secrets of their worth.
Rustling leaves, a gentle song,
In this stillness, we belong.

Twilight dances, shadows cast,
Moments fleeting, gone so fast.
Every breath, a world apart,
Echoes linger in the heart.

Snowflakes drift with soft descent,
Marking where the shadows went.
In the quiet, hope will rise,
Beneath the weight of winter skies.

Among the trees, we stand and wait,
Listening close to fate's debate.
Every sigh, a story spun,
In barren woods, the warmth begun.

Revelations in the Glare

Amidst the light, reflections gleam,
Chasing shadows, lost in dream.
Every shimmer tells a tale,
In the bright, the storm will wail.

Raindrops glisten on the street,
Dancing rhythms, soft and sweet.
Brightened paths reveal our fears,
In the glare, we shed our tears.

Mirrors mask the truth we seek,
In bold light, we feel the weak.
But through the haze, a vision glows,
In every heart, a spark still grows.

Underground, the roots entwine,
Seeking strength in dark divine.
Beneath the glare, we find our song,
In the light, we all belong.

Revelations dance like flame,
In the torchlight, call our name.
Brightly burning, hearts aligned,
In the glare, our strength defined.

The Moon's Frigid Caress

The moonlit glow on frozen lakes,
Whispers secrets, softly breaks.
A silver touch on winter's breath,
In quiet peace, we wandereth.

Shadows dance in the pale moonlight,
Stars peek through, a wondrous sight.
The world, in slumber, wrapped in white,
Holds its dreams until the night.

Each flake of snow, a fleeting kiss,
The tranquil air, a moment's bliss.
Beneath its gaze, hearts intertwine,
In the embrace of cold divine.

A time of stillness, a time of grace,
With every glance, a soft embrace.
The moon above, our silent friend,
In its glow, all sorrows mend.

As dawn approaches, shadows flee,
Leaving behind a memory.
In the cold light, warmth shall grow,
Thanks to the moon's soft, frigid glow.

Luminous Frost

I wander through a realm of white,
Where frost ignites the morning light.
Each blade of grass, a crystal gem,
In this enchanting, frozen hem.

The air is crisp, the silence deep,
Nature's promise, her secrets keep.
A tapestry of ice unfurls,
In perfect harmony, it twirls.

Luminous frost on windowpanes,
Captures all the joy that reigns.
A fleeting spell, a moment's grace,
In the stillness, we find our place.

As sunlight kisses icy trails,
A dance of light, the magic sails.
With every glance, the world does gleam,
In nature's heart, we chase the dream.

So let us walk this frosty way,
Where winter's chill turns night to day.
In luminous frost, our spirits soar,
A beautiful world forevermore.

Veil of the Glacial Night

Beneath the stars, the earth runs cold,
A tale of dreams, in whispers told.
A veil of frost, so pure and bright,
Enfolds the world within the night.

In shadows deep, the chill does creep,
Where secrets hide and silence weeps.
The moon, a guardian high above,
Watches o'er with timeless love.

The trees stand tall, their branches bare,
Embracing stillness, entranced in air.
Each breath of night a gentle sigh,
In the glacial tale, we learn to fly.

A dance of silence, the heartbeats slow,
In nature's arms, all troubles go.
We wander free in this vast expanse,
In glacial night, we find our chance.

With every step, the frost does gleam,
A quiet spell, a lingering dream.
In the veil of night, we come alive,
Where hopes converge and spirits thrive.

Shimmering Stars through the Boughs

Through tangled boughs, the stars do peek,
A hidden world, both bright and meek.
With every twinkle, stories share,
Of distant lands, of dreams laid bare.

The gentle rustle of the leaves,
Whispers tales that nature weaves.
In midnight's hush, the heart does sing,
Of love remembered and hope's wings.

The silver glow plays hide and seek,
Among the trees, both tall and sleek.
My soul ignites with every star,
Guiding my thoughts, no matter how far.

In the cool embrace of night so deep,
In shimmering light, I find my peace.
Each moment, a gift, forever bright,
In nature's hand, all feels right.

So let us wander through the night,
Beneath the stars, our hearts take flight.
In the dance of life, we join the throng,
And find our place, where we belong.

Mysteries of the Nightfall Chill

Whispers curl in the chilled air,
Beneath the moon's soft, silver glare.
Shadows stretch and softly creep,
In darkened corners, secrets sleep.

The pines sway with a haunting song,
Where night's enchantments drift along.
Faint echoes of forgotten dreams,
Float like mist on silver beams.

Stars blink with a knowing grace,
Hiding tales in their embrace.
The chill wraps tight around the heart,
Inviting souls to play their part.

Dew-kissed grass reflects the light,
Awakening wonder in the night.
A world alive, yet still and deep,
In nightfall's arm, we gently leap.

Mysteries wrapped in shadows weave,
A tapestry that beckons, leave.
In night's still grasp, we find our way,
Guided by stars until the day.

Dancer of the Starry Light

Under the canopy of starlit glow,
A dancer moves, light and slow.
Each step a whisper, each twirl a dream,
In harmony with the silver stream.

Her silken dress flows like the night,
As she twirls under the moon's soft light.
With every leap, the cosmos sighs,
Unveiling magic in darkened skies.

In the vastness, she knows no fear,
Her laughter echoes, bright and clear.
Each star a partner in her flight,
Illuminating the canvas of night.

As comets streak, her spirit soars,
Awakening wonder behind closed doors.
To dance among the cosmic lore,
Is to give the heavens what they crave for.

In the stillness, she finds her grace,
Woven in time, a cosmic embrace.
A dancer lost in the starry tide,
In every heartbeat, the universe sighed.

Secrets Wrapped in Snowflakes

Upon the ground, soft secrets lay,
Each snowflake whispers, come what may.
A tapestry of white unfolds,
In frosty breath, the world beholds.

Hushed whispers ride the winter's air,
Echoes of dreams, tender and rare.
Nature's artistry, pure and bright,
Crafted in silence, a shimmering sight.

Every flake a tale untold,
In frozen layers, mysteries hold.
As daylight dances on icy streams,
The heart recalls fading dreams.

Children laugh, their joy a song,
In winter's arms, we all belong.
Together we weave, layer by layer,
A world adorned with dreams and care.

In frosty whispers, the secrets lie,
Beneath the gray, a hopeful sky.
As snowflakes fall, they gently tease,
Inviting wonder, bringing peace.

Pristine Nights Under a Shimmering Veil

Under the stars, a silence reigns,
A pristine night where calm remains.
Softly the world in shadows glows,
Wrapped in mysteries, nobody knows.

The veil of night, a gossamer thread,
Where dreams awaken, fears are shed.
Whispers of moonlight kiss the land,
A touch of magic, gentle and grand.

In stillness, hearts begin to race,
Finding solace in twilight's embrace.
Each breath a moment, pure and free,
A dance with time and eternity.

Stars twinkle like fairy dust,
In this night, we place our trust.
Through the quiet, spirits soar,
Exploring realms forevermore.

In joy and peace, the night unveils,
Stories hidden behind soft trails.
Beneath the dome where wishes sail,
We are enchanted, under a shimmering veil.

Enchanted Nightfall

The stars awake, a gentle tune,
Whispers carried by the moon.
In shadows deep, the secrets play,
As dreams emerge, they drift away.

The breeze it dances, soft and light,
Caressing souls, igniting night.
With every breath, the magic swells,
In hidden paths where silence dwells.

Glimmers sparkle on the ground,
In this enchanted world we've found.
Where time stands still and hearts ignite,
Beneath the spell of pure delight.

The forest hums a lullaby,
As fireflies flicker in the sky.
Lost in wonder, hand in hand,
Together, we will understand.

Soon dawn will break, the magic fade,
Yet in our hearts, it won't evade.
For in the night, our spirits thrall,
In every breath, enchanted call.

The Pale Watcher Above

In the stillness, shadows cling,
The pale watcher begins to sing.
Eyes like lanterns in the void,
Guarding dreams that night deployed.

Whispers echo through the trees,
Carried softly by the breeze.
A presence felt, an ancient guide,
In secret realms where phantoms bide.

With every chill that wraps the night,
The pale watcher brings delight.
A silhouette against the stars,
Binding souls with distant scars.

In twilight's hold, we seek the truth,
Innocence lost, the spark of youth.
Yet as we gaze upon the hue,
The watcher smiles, embracing you.

As dawn approaches, shadows wane,
But the pale watcher will remain.
In hearts aglow, a whispered vow,
To keep the secrets of the now.

Crystal Veils of the Night

Beneath the moon's soft silver gleam,
The world appears like a stolen dream.
Crystal veils in shadows spin,
Inviting all the magic in.

With every step, the night unfurls,
Revealing hidden, secret swirls.
In every glance, the spirits rise,
Dancing softly 'neath starry skies.

The air is thick with mystic scents,
Bringing peace and new intents.
Each breath a promise, each sigh a plea,
In the veil of night, we feel so free.

Softly now, the darkness sings,
Enveloping us in gentle wings.
We reach for moments like starlit dew,
In crystal veils, our dreams come true.

And as the dawn's first light breaks through,
The magic lingers, faint yet true.
For in our hearts, that veil of night,
Will forever be our guiding light.

Onyric Chill

When twilight whispers through the air,
An onyric chill begins to flare.
With every breath, the shadows grow,
Revealing secrets we don't know.

In corridors of mist and haze,
We wander lost in endless maze.
The chill of night, a haunting balm,
Cradles all in its eerie calm.

Echoes haunt with gentle sighs,
As phantoms dance beneath dark skies.
The chill is sharp, the night is deep,
In dreams we weave, awake we sleep.

Yet fear not the shadows that creep,
For in their depths, the silence keeps.
We learn to roam, to trust the fall,
In onyric chill, we find our call.

As dawn approaches, shadows fade,
But night will come, unafraid.
In icy breaths, the chill remains,
A whispered promise, through the plains.

Frostbitten Dreams

In winter's grip, the world stands still,
A canvas white, the air is chill.
Each breath a cloud, each step a crunch,
In silent woods, the heart will munch.

The whispers carry through the pines,
A frosty tale, where magic twines.
Stars glimmer down in sapphire hues,
While shadows dance in frosty blues.

Beneath the moon's enchanted glow,
The dreams unfold, a wondrous show.
They drift like snowflakes, soft and light,
In frosted dreams that pierce the night.

Each fleeting thought, a fragile flake,
A moment's warmth we cannot take.
Yet still we cling to visions bright,
In frostbitten dreams, we find our flight.

So let the cold embrace the night,
For in its depths, we find our light.
In frosty realms where dreams align,
We seek the warmth of hearts divine.

The Stillness of Starlit Quiet

Under a blanket, vast and deep,
The stars above like secrets keep.
In stillness wrapped, the world's at rest,
The night reveals its silent quest.

A whisper travels through the air,
Each twinkle holds a timeless prayer.
In gentle hush, the moments fade,
As starlit dreams are softly laid.

Moonbeams dance on sleeping stones,
While shadows hum their ancient tones.
The calm of night, a serenade,
In stillness, wonders are conveyed.

With every breath, the night unfolds,
A tapestry of dreams retold.
In quietude, our spirits fly,
Beneath the veil of starlit sky.

So pause awhile, let worries cease,
In starlit quiet, find your peace.
For in this moment, hearts unite,
And bask in beauty, pure delight.

Shadows on Crystal Lakes

Reflections dance upon the shore,
As twilight whispers, seeking more.
The crystal lake, a mirror pure,
Holds secrets deep, and dreams demure.

Beneath the trees where shadows play,
In evening's grasp, the light will sway.
Each ripple tells of tales untold,
A canvas bright with hues of gold.

As darkened forms begin to blend,
The day retreats, the night ascends.
Stars shimmer soft on water's face,
In tranquil grace, we find our place.

The whispering winds embrace the night,
While shadows stretch in soft twilight.
A sacred bond, this space we share,
Where spirits wander, light as air.

So linger here, in this embrace,
Where shadows on the lake leave trace.
For in this calm, our souls shall wake,
To blend with dreams on crystal lakes.

Whispering Cold Light

In the hush of dawn, where shadows flee,
The world awakens, wild and free.
Cold light whispers, soft and low,
Painting the earth with a silver glow.

The frost-kissed leaves gleam in the sun,
A fleeting moment, soft and fun.
Each ray that breaks, a promise made,
In whispering light, the night will fade.

Across the fields, a tranquil breeze,
Carries the secrets of ancient trees.
With every shiver, life ignites,
In the tender glow of cold light's bites.

So let the morning wrap you tight,
In dreams awakened by the light.
For in each whisper, hope resides,
In cold light's embrace, our joy abides.

As day unfolds, and night takes flight,
We find our way in cold light's sight.
With hearts aglow, we rise and cheer,
In the whispering cold, we hold what's dear.

Frosted Dreams in Twilight

In twilight's glow, the shadows creep,
A whisper soft, as the world falls deep.
Frost on petals, a crystalline kiss,
In dreams of winter, we find our bliss.

Glistening stars in the evening's sigh,
Painted skies where the cold winds fly.
Each breath a cloud, a silent song,
In frosted dreams, we know we belong.

The moonlight dances on fields of white,
A tranquil hush, a pure delight.
Footprints vanish, as if they know,
The secrets kept in the softest snow.

Beneath the branches, the silver steals,
Warming hearts where the cold reveals.
In every flake, a story spun,
As twilight fades, we become one.

So let us wander, hand in hand,
Through frosted dreams in a quiet land.
As twilight whispers its sweet refrain,
In frozen beauty, we will remain.

Lunar Whispers of Cold Nights

The moon hangs low in the velvet sky,
Casting shadows where the cold winds sigh.
With every step, the frost crisps clear,
Lunar whispers, so soft and near.

A blanket thick, the night unfurls,
Glistening softly, a quilt of pearls.
Echoes linger in the icy air,
Carried by silence, a secret shared.

Faint stars twinkle, like distant dreams,
Reflected in frost, a dance that gleams.
Beneath the boughs where the nightbirds sing,
Lunar tales of the peace they bring.

Every breath becomes a shimmering mist,
Moments fleeting, so easily missed.
In cold embrace, we softly tread,
Guided by whispers that linger ahead.

Under the heavens, our hearts ignite,
In the calm of these cold, starry nights.
The moon's soft glow leads the way anew,
With lunar whispers, all feels true.

Sibilant Snowfall Serenade

Snowflakes twirl in a gentle dance,
A sibilant serenade in winter's trance.
Whispers of magic as they softly land,
Creating a canvas, a quiet land.

Each flake unique, a delicate art,
Falling with grace to warm the heart.
A lullaby sung by the winds of old,
As stories of winter begin to unfold.

Crystalline crystals spark the night,
Reflecting dreams in a world of white.
In the hush of snow, we find our peace,
Sibilant serenades that never cease.

Nature's symphony, soft and sweet,
A melody wrapped in the chill we greet.
With every flake, a moment to hold,
In the serene embrace of the frosty cold.

So let us wander through this pure bliss,
In snow's quiet dance, nothing amiss.
As the world sleeps beneath this shade,
We find our song in the snowfall's cascade.

Celestial Chill

In the stillness of night, the air feels thin,
A celestial chill that wraps us in.
Stars shimmer faintly, like dreams in flight,
Guiding our hearts through the endless night.

Frosted whispers in the moon's soft glow,
We trace the patterns where the echoes flow.
Each shimmering breath, a moment we steal,
In the depth of the dark, we learn to feel.

The world is aglow with a silver hue,
As if the cosmos has painted anew.
Cradled by darkness, we find our way,
In celestial chill, we wish to stay.

Time slows down as the night grows deep,
In the cradle of silence, our secrets keep.
Wrapped in the chill, our spirits soar,
In the calm of the night, we long for more.

Together we wander through shadows cast,
In the celestial chill, we find our past.
As dreams take flight on the wings of air,
In this tranquil beauty, we find our care.

Shimmering Shadows on Ice

Beneath the moon's soft glow,
The frozen pond reflects dreams,
Shadows dance with the night,
In whispers, the cold sun gleams.

Nature's breath, a hushed sigh,
Crystal shards catch the light,
Gliding spirits hover near,
In this realm, pure and bright.

Winds weave tales of the past,
Each flake tells a story old,
As laughter rides on the breeze,
A tapestry, woven bold.

Footsteps echo on the glass,
Imprints fade with the night's breath,
In shimmering layers, we glide,
A ballet 'twixt life and death.

So here we stand, hand in hand,
In this frozen, transient space,
Shimmering shadows write our fate,
As time drapes us in lace.

Ethereal Light Among the Pines

Dappled rays break through the leaves,
Whispering secrets to the ground,
In this haven, peace weaves,
A tapestry without a sound.

Pine needles carpet the earth,
Softly cradling every step,
Gentle breezes hold their mirth,
In this realm where spirits slept.

Mossy trunks stand guard so tall,
Guardians of tales untold,
Greeting wanderers who call,
To the stories wrapped in gold.

Crickets sing as dusk embraces,
A lullaby for stars above,
In the stillness, time effaces,
Our worries, cradled in love.

Here, under the celestial dome,
Ethereal light paints the sky,
Among the pines, we find home,
Where dreams and nature fly.

Nocturnal Gem Amongst the Frost

In the velvet of the night,
A gem glimmers, bright and rare,
Mist enfolds it, soft as light,
A vision caught in icy air.

Stars twinkle through the stillness,
Each breath forms a fleeting cloud,
Nature wraps all in chillness,
From silence, hearts grow loud.

Beneath a canopy of dark,
Whispers ride on frozen streams,
Guided by a single spark,
In dreams, we chase the seams.

Frosted petals, delicate, frail,
Capture night's most tender kiss,
A languid dance, no sound, no wail,
In this moment, purest bliss.

Nocturnal gem, soft and bright,
Hold us in your gentle gaze,
As the world succumbs to night,
In wonder, we lose our ways.

Starlit Silence in the Frost

A blanket of stars, silvery white,
Covers the earth in whispers low,
As the frost bites with gentle might,
Nature hums in a tranquil flow.

In the heart of a winter's night,
Silence sings a sweet refrain,
Footsteps fade in the soft twilight,
Echoes linger, like soft rain.

The moon weaves dreams on the ground,
Casting shadows, fragile and sleek,
In the distance, no voice found,
Just the stillness, rare and meek.

Frozen breaths form delicate lace,
As wonder paints the world anew,
In starlit silence, we embrace,
Every shimmering timeworn view.

So let the night cradle our fears,
In this frosty, enchanted space,
With every twinkle, laughter nears,
In starlit silence, find our place.

Glistening Dreams Beneath a Pale Sky

In whispers soft the dreams take flight,
They dance upon the edge of night.
Stars twinkle gently, a silver sigh,
Beneath the vast and watchful sky.

Each moment glistens like morning dew,
Hopes awaken, fresh and new.
Through fields of gold, they gently weave,
In the stillness, we believe.

Embers flicker as shadows play,
Chasing twilight, fading day.
With every breath, a wish is spun,
In this realm, we are all one.

Stories whispered in hushed tones,
Carried softly on time's own bones.
Beneath the pale, enchanting dome,
We find our hearts, our dreams, our home.

Awake within this dreamlike haze,
Caught in wonder, lost in gaze.
The world glimmers with secrets untold,
In twilight's arms, our spirits unfold.

Echoes of Stillness

In the heart of silence, secrets lie,
Softly sighing beneath a wide sky.
Whispers travel like gentle streams,
Carrying softly the weight of dreams.

Nature holds her breath in calm,
A tranquil world, a soothing balm.
Moments linger, time feels vast,
In echoes of stillness, shadows cast.

Leaves rustle with stories of old,
Mysteries wrapped in green and gold.
Each pause is filled with hidden grace,
In stillness we find a sacred space.

A gentle breeze begins to weave,
Through the heart, we learn to believe.
In whispered tones, the earth will speak,
To those who listen, to souls unique.

Amidst the calm, a feeling grows,
Awakening paths the spirit knows.
With open hearts and mindful ways,
We cherish life's unspoken praise.

A Tapestry of White and Light

Threads of white in morning glow,
Stitch the fabric of dreams below.
With every stitch, a story weaves,
In the heart, the spirit believes.

In fields where snowflakes softly fall,
Nature whispers, beckons all.
Every crystal, a wish alight,
In this tapestry of white and light.

A canvas laid where shadows play,
Night gives way to the break of day.
Every dawn, a work of art,
In the fabric, we find our heart.

Glimmers sparkle in winter's breath,
Life reborn, a dance with death.
Each moment captures the fleeting spark,
In the beauty, we leave our mark.

As colors blend in twilight's fold,
Life's stories breathe, alive and bold.
Together woven, pure delight,
In the tapestry of white and light.

Glacial Reflections

In icy whispers, the world stands still,
Glaciers gleam upon the hill.
Mirrored surfaces, secrets hold,
Time etched deep in shades of cold.

With every crack, a timeless song,
Echoing where the heart belongs.
Chasms whisper tales of old,
In frozen realms, the truth unfolds.

Silence reigns in frosted air,
Nature's canvas, pure and rare.
Beneath the ice, a heart beats strong,
A melody of right and wrong.

Infinite beauty wrapped in chill,
With every glance, we seek to fill.
In glacial reflections, we find peace,
A moment's pause, a sweet release.

Capturing light in frozen streams,
Glacial reflections, untouched dreams.
In nature's grasp, we each belong,
In harmony, we sing our song.

Charles of Cold

In winter's grasp, he walks alone,
The crisp air chills, a whispered tone.
His footsteps echo, soft and clear,
A lonely path, but never fear.

With frost-kissed breath, he paints the dawn,
Each flake a jewel on lawns withdrawn.
His heart is warm, though the world is cold,
In solitude, his stories unfold.

Beneath the stars, he finds his muse,
In shadows deep, he will not lose.
A frostbitten joy, a silent art,
In every chill, he finds his heart.

The moonlight dances on silver streams,
Awakening hopes, igniting dreams.
Charles of Cold, in night's embrace,
Finds endless beauty in empty space.

So let the world outside be frayed,
In each cold breath, a bond is made.
The winter's chill, a friend to keep,
In the stillness, memories sleep.

Resplendent Silence in the Dark

Under the stars, where shadows play,
Resplendent silence holds sway.
The world, a canvas, stark and bright,
Whispers secrets in the night.

Each breath of wind, a gentle sigh,
The moon a guardian in the sky.
In this hush, all thoughts align,
A peace profound, both rare and fine.

Dreams unfurl in velvet tones,
A symphony of silent moans.
The darkness wraps, a soft embrace,
In every corner, stillness traces.

What mysteries does the night conceal?
In quietude, our hearts can heal.
Each heartbeat echoes, loud and clear,
In resplendent silence, we draw near.

A tapestry of stars adorns,
The secret whispers of the morns.
In this calm, we find our way,
In resplendent silence, we shall stay.

Elysian Frost

In the morning light, a shimmer bright,
Elysian frost dances with delight.
Each crystal blooms, a fleeting sight,
Nature's wonder, pure and white.

Glistening fields, a magical show,
Where dreams awaken, soft and slow.
The air is crisp, the world aglow,
In this embrace, our spirits grow.

Frosted branches, like silver lace,
Hold every moment, a tender grace.
In every breath, a story spun,
Beneath the frost, the warmth of sun.

Time stands still in this ethereal space,
Elysian frost, a gentle embrace.
With each step taken on this path,
Joy blooms forth, igniting a laugh.

In the hush of dawn, where wonders meet,
Nature's lullaby, so calm and sweet.
Elysian frost, forever we chase,
A fleeting glimpse of heaven's face.

Cradled in Lunar Hues

The moonlight bathes the sleeping earth,
In gentle shades of tranquil mirth.
Cradled in lunar hues so bright,
Whispers of dreams take graceful flight.

Silver beams on the silent glade,
Casting shadows where secrets wade.
In this glow, the world feels new,
Wrapped in the essence of night's view.

Each star a witness, shining bold,
To stories of love and hopes retold.
In lunar hues, our spirits soar,
Embracing enchantment forevermore.

The night unfolds, a canvas bare,
Where soul and stars entwine with care.
Cradled softly in dreams so true,
In the serenade of the moon's hue.

Time whispers soft on this blessed night,
In lunar hues, all feels right.
With every heartbeat, the cosmos calls,
Cradled in dreams, where magic falls.

Shadows Danced in Glacial Light

In twilight's breath, the shadows play,
Their silhouettes in soft array.
Underneath the frozen haze,
They weave their paths in silent ways.

A flicker here, a glimmer there,
Dancing whispers fill the air.
Among the trees, the echoes roam,
In glacial light, they find their home.

Waltzing on the icy ground,
With every step, a haunting sound.
Ephemeral, yet so profound,
In such a chill, warmth can be found.

They twirl and fade, a fleeting sight,
In the vastness of the night.
As frost begins to kiss the leaves,
The magic lingers, then it leaves.

Yet in the still, they seem to breathe,
As moonlit dreams weave and seethe.
The glacial whispers softly call,
In shadows' dance, we feel it all.

A Shimmer above the Snowdrift

Beneath the stars, a glimmer bright,
A shimmer glows with pure delight.
Above the drifts of soft white snow,
A quiet presence, gentle flow.

It sparkles where the cold winds sigh,
As winter birds above them fly.
In silence deep, a beauty lies,
With twinkling hues that mesmerize.

The moon spills light on icy streams,
Awakening the night with dreams.
Where snowflakes dance in frosty air,
The shimmer sings of magic rare.

With every breath the night takes pause,
In tranquil peace, life finds its cause.
A world of white, serene and deep,
In starlit night, the heavens weep.

Yet hidden in that gentle glow,
A secret lies, a tale to show,
Of winter's grip, both fierce and light,
In shimmer's heart, the world feels right.

Specter of a Quiet Glow

In shadows deep, a specter's stride,
A quiet glow where dreams abide.
Among the folds of night's embrace,
It wanders softly, leaving grace.

With every step, the silence stirs,
In whispered notes, the stillness purrs.
A light that flickers, dim yet clear,
The specter's touch brings hidden cheer.

It haunts the corners of the mind,
In every secret, truth we find.
Like stars that shimmer from afar,
A gentle guide, a wishing star.

From shadows cast, the glow appears,
Embracing hopes, dispelling fears.
Within its warmth, lost souls unite,
In quiet realms where dreams take flight.

So linger long, embrace the shade,
In spectral light, let worries fade.
For in this place, all hearts may grow,
With tender love, a quiet glow.

Suspended in Icy Serenity

In frozen stillness, time stands still,
A world encased in winter's chill.
Suspended high, the crystal trees,
Adorned with snow that bends the breeze.

The air is crisp, the whispers soft,
As flakes cascade and gently loft.
In icy clarity, the night,
Reveals its secrets, bathed in light.

A tranquil peace, a sacred hush,
Where nature's beauty calls, a rush.
The stars gaze down with jeweled grace,
In this serene, enchanted place.

Amidst the silence, hearts align,
With every breath, the world divine.
Suspended here, we find our peace,
In icy arms, our worries cease.

So take a moment, breathe it in,
Allow the calm, let joy begin.
For in this still, pure, lovely land,
We find the warmth of nature's hand.

Shadows in the Glimmering White

In the stillness of winter's embrace,
Shadows dance softly, a delicate trace.
Moonlight glimmers on frostbitten ground,
In silence, the world wraps softly around.

Footsteps linger in the pale, crisp air,
Ghostly whispers weave through the midnight stare.
Trees stand as sentinels, long and deep,
Guarding secrets that winter will keep.

The nightingale sings a muted refrain,
Each note carries echoes of joy and pain.
Stars blink gently, like eyes in a dream,
Reflections shimmer, a glistening stream.

Beneath the blanket of snow, hearts remain,
Warm memories thaw the cold's metallic chain.
In the shadows, hope lies patiently, wait,
For the dawn to break free, resolute fate.

The world unfolds in a shimmering shroud,
Caught between silence, serene but loud.
In the glow of the night, whispers take flight,
With shadows that dance in the glimmering white.

Celestial Embrace of Solitude

In the still sky where stars softly breathe,
Loneliness gathers, a cloak to seethe.
Planets twirl silently, lost in their dance,
While the heart beats softly, caught in a trance.

The moon, a guardian, whispers so low,
Embracing the spirit in its silver glow.
Clouds drift like thoughts in a gentle stream,
Cradling the dreams that dark hours may glean.

Above, the universe stretches its hand,
Cradling the silence like grains of sand.
In solitude's arms, one learns to find peace,
In the cosmic expanse, heart's burdens cease.

Each constellation tells tales of despair,
Yet in their quiet, a soft, sweet prayer.
For in the night's solitude, one may recall,
A celestial embrace that cradles us all.

Through galaxies vast, the soul finds its thread,
Woven in silence, where all fears are shed.
In the stillness, beauty forever remains,
In the celestial embrace that solitude gains.

The Luminous Silence

In quiet corners where shadows play,
Luminous silence guides the way.
Glints of starlight, a whisper of grace,
Filling the void, a tender embrace.

Moonbeams drape softly on slumbering trees,
Cradling the night in a gentle freeze.
Each breath of the dark holds a secret right,
In the depth of stillness, ignites the night.

Amidst the quiet, thoughts take to flight,
Carried by dreams into the soft night.
Echoes of stillness collide and convene,
In the tapestry woven from what might have been.

With every heartbeat, the silence expands,
Filling the mind with vast, open lands.
The luminous glow of the stars appears,
Soothing the heart, dissolving all fears.

In the embrace of the dark, one can grow,
Finding strength where the soft breezes blow.
In luminous silence, we often find peace,
Moments of wonder, where troubles cease.

Chill Breath of Emergent Night

As twilight descends, the chill sets in,
Whispers of night call, a soft violin.
Stars peek from shadows, a shimmering sight,
Beneath the vast canvas of emerging night.

The air, crisp with secrets, breathes deep,
Awakening thoughts from the day's gentle sleep.
In silence, the world holds its breath in pause,
To witness the wonders, to ruminate cause.

Beneath the tapestry, life holds its thread,
Colors of twilight dance, softly spread.
Each moment a heartbeat, so fragile yet bright,
In the cool embrace of the emergent night.

With every gust of wind, echoes arise,
Stories forgotten beneath starlit skies.
The chill wraps around like a shawl, so tight,
Cradling all under the cloak of night.

In the heart of the dark, dreams find their form,
Rising like tides in the cloak of the storm.
For in the chill breath, magic ignites,
Transforming the world in the emergent night.

Dreaming in Frosty Silence

In the still of night, whispers fade,
Dreams weave soft in a snow-white glade.
Stars twinkle gently, a silver balm,
Wrapped in chill, the world's a calm.

Frosted branches, a delicate lace,
Hushed by winter, the world finds grace.
Moonlight dances on frozen streams,
In this silence, we hold our dreams.

Footprints vanish in a crystalline swirl,
Nature's beauty, a quiet pearl.
Each breath visible, a cloud of thought,
In this moment, all worries are caught.

Time drifts softly, as shadows merge,
In this realm, our souls surge.
Whispers of hope in the cold air,
In frosty silence, we linger there.

Chilling Luminance

Beneath the frost, a light does glow,
Sparkling softly on fields of snow.
Each flake a gem, a wondrous sight,
In chilling luminance, hearts take flight.

Shadows play in the winter's gleam,
A frozen landscape, a tranquil dream.
Glistening crystals crown the trees,
Whispering secrets on the frosty breeze.

The quiet hum of a snowy night,
Glows in the dark, pure and bright.
In this embrace of shivering light,
Hope ignites with the coming night.

As dawn breaks soft, the chill retreats,
A symphony of silence, nature's beats.
In every sparkle a story's spun,
In chilling luminance, life's just begun.

Echoes of the Glacial Radiance

In the heart of winter, echoes sing,
Of glacial radiance, a wondrous thing.
Whispers travel on the icy air,
Carried gently, a tale to share.

Mountains rise in a frozen embrace,
Glistening softly, nature's grace.
Every sound is crisp and clear,
In these echoes, we draw near.

Footsteps crunch on the blanket white,
Each moment glows in the soft twilight.
Reflections cast on a mirrored lake,
In glacial silence, our hearts awake.

The world feels paused, in stillness vast,
Memories linger, shadows cast.
In every echo, a story grows,
In glacial radiance, peace flows.

As the sun sets, colors flare,
Painting the sky with beauty rare.
In this reverie, we find our place,
In echoes of the glacial space.

Twilight's Frosted Whisper

In twilight's glow, the world is hushed,
Frosted whispers, softly brushed.
Shadows dance on a silvery field,
In this moment, our hearts revealed.

The sky embers in purple and gold,
A tale of winter begins to unfold.
Each breath carries a frosty tune,
As stars awaken beneath the moon.

Branches glisten in the fading light,
Nature's canvas, a stunning sight.
Winds carry secrets through the night,
In twilight's whisper, all feels right.

The world is wrapped in a soft embrace,
Time slows down in this sacred space.
In every flurry, the night sings low,
Twilight's frosted whispers, a gentle flow.

As darkness deepens, dreams arise,
Woven in magic beneath the skies.
In this stillness, our souls entwine,
In twilight whispers, all is divine.

The Soft Glow Abroad

A gentle light spills forth,
Casting dreams upon the ground.
Whispering secrets of the night,
With every shadow, joy is found.

Stars shimmer like distant wishes,
In the velvet of deep skies.
Echoes of laughter linger,
As the world softly sighs.

Moonbeams dance on tranquil streams,
Guiding souls through evening's grace.
In the stillness, hope awaits,
A warm and tender embrace.

Soft winds carry fragrant blooms,
Each petal a story untold.
In this glow, lives intertwine,
As night bids dreams to unfold.

So let the soft glow lead you,
To where the heart finds peace.
Among the stars shimmering bright,
May your worries find release.

Dark Canvas Adorned in Light

A canvas black, void of scene,
Yet splashed with colors so bold.
Galaxies twirl in silent dance,
As mysteries and tales unfold.

Each stroke breathes whispers of life,
Painting dreams on endless nights.
Hues of hope amidst despair,
Creating warmth with flickered lights.

Dark shades cradle every spark,
A contrast of shadows and gleams.
In the silence, the heart ignites,
With flickers of daring dreams.

Behold the beauty of the unknown,
Where fear and wonder coexist.
Amidst the stillness, stories wake,
Their voices heard, they can't resist.

Stars serve as brushes above,
Painting worlds with twilight's kiss.
In this realm of night and light,
Find solace in the peaceful bliss.

So gaze upon this wondrous sight,
Embrace the dance of day and night.

Dusk's Icy Embrace

Dusk descends with chilling grace,
Wrapping all in its cool arms.
The sun surrenders to the night,
Carrying with it, its warm charms.

Frosted whispers fill the air,
As shadows stretch across the earth.
Moments pause, their breath held tight,
In the stillness, echoes of mirth.

Stars shiver in the evening's chill,
Glistening like crystals in black.
Nature rests, its heart beats slow,
As the world wraps in its cloak, intact.

The moon climbs high, a silver sphere,
Casting dreams on every face.
Each soul finds peace in night's cool breath,
Awakening to dusk's embrace.

In this quiet, hearts can mend,
Night's beauty so softly creates.
A promise held in icy still,
For dawn's return, as night abates.

Silver-Hued Tranquility

A silver veil drapes over trees,
Silent whispers in the air.
Moonlight flows like gentle streams,
Glistening on each branch laid bare.

Softly basking in night's glow,
The world finds peace in stillness found.
Every heartbeat echoes calm,
In this serene and sacred ground.

Reflections dance on placid lakes,
Where ripples weave a tranquil ballet.
In the quiet, dreams ignite,
As silver silver threads softly sway.

Time stretches like the twilight fog,
Wrapping souls in its embrace.
In this hush, the heart unfolds,
Finding joy in the gentle space.

So linger here beneath the stars,
Let tranquility soothe your mind.
In silver hues, may you discover,
The beauty in the night unwind.

Whispers of the Frigid Moonlight

In the stillness of the night,
The moon casts a silver glow,
Whispers travel on the breeze,
Secrets only shadows know.

Beneath the gaze of starry skies,
Hearts entwined in hushed delight,
Echoes linger with soft sighs,
Lost in the frigid moonlight.

Crisp the air, a tender chill,
Nature speaks in muted tones,
Every rustle, every thrill,
A symphony of heartbeats, alone.

Glistening frost upon the leaves,
Glimmers like a dreamer's tear,
In this moment, one believes,
Magic lingers, pure and clear.

So let us dance beneath the beams,
Drawn by whispers, pale and bright,
Wrapped in warmth of frozen dreams,
Together, lost in moonlit night.

Cloaked in Frost's Embrace

Nature's blanket, soft and white,
Cloaked in frost's gentle grace,
Every branch a crystal sight,
Time slows down in this embrace.

Footsteps crunch on frozen ground,
Echoes fade in winter's breath,
In this world, beauty found,
Chilled whispers speak of life and death.

Icicles hang like fragile art,
Painting scenes of quietude,
In the stillness, warms the heart,
Frost creates its own solitude.

Beneath this calm, a pulse awaits,
Life beneath the winter's skin,
Nature patiently contemplates,
When the warmth of spring begins.

Glimmering under pale moon's light,
Frosted dreams come alive and dance,
In this moment, pure and bright,
Each breath sparks a timeless romance.

Murmurs Beneath a Pale Shimmer

Underneath the quiet glow,
Murmurs sweep through fading trees,
A whispered tale, soft and slow,
Carried lightly on the breeze.

Moonlit dew hangs on each blade,
Tales of night entwined with dreams,
In the shadows, magic played,
Life transforms at twilight's seams.

Faint reflections, silvery sheen,
Every rustle holds a truth,
Beneath the pale, a world unseen,
Capturing the essence of youth.

In this whispering embrace,
Night reveals its hidden charms,
A dance of light, a lover's grace,
Luring souls into its arms.

And as the stars begin to fade,
Murmurs linger, soft and light,
In the heart where dreams are laid,
Life's tender song takes flight.

Dreams in the Luminescent Chill

In the chill of a crisp night,
Dreams unfold like gentle snow,
Each flake whispers of delight,
In this glow where magic flows.

Stars above like scattered seeds,
Planting wishes, hopes anew,
In this silence, heart now bleeds,
Longing for the light we knew.

Every breath forms clouds of thought,
In the air, a warmth ignites,
In the depths, a peace is sought,
Wrapped in dreams, lost in the lights.

Luminescent paths await,
Guiding brave souls through the night,
Every journey, love or fate,
Draws us near, ignites the flight.

So let us wander, hand in hand,
Through the chill, our spirits blend,
In this dreamlike winter land,
Where chilly whispers never end.

Milton Keynes UK
Ingram Content Group UK Ltd.
UKHW021045031224
452078UK00010B/589